BEST DIPS & APPS EVER

D1444370

BEST
DIPS &
APPS
EVER

FUN AND EASY SPREADS, SNACKS, AND SAVORY BITES

MONICA SWEENEY

Page 1, 8, 31, 45: © Sarsmis/iStockphoto.com; 10, 11: © Funwithfood/iStockphoto.com; 12, 16, 20, 27, 32, 33, 37, 38, 61, 67, 87, 108, 111: © bhofack2/iStockphoto.com; 15: © Lesyy/iStockphoto.com; 19: © Wiktory/iStockphoto.com; 23, 34, 49, 51, 59, 75, 77, 84, 89, 94, 97, 98, 101, 107: © Lauri Patterson/iStockphoto.com; 24, 28, 41, 121, 122: © cobra-photo/iStockphoto.com; 42: © Petar Chernaev/iStockphoto.com; 46: © MrKornFlakes/iStockphoto.com; 52: © PeteerS/iStockphoto.com; 54, 55: © Kevin Landwer-Johan/iStockphoto.com; 56: © Teleginatania/iStockphoto.com; 62: © Azurita/iStockphoto.com; 65: © nata_vkusidey/iStockphoto.com; 66: © AlenaKogotkova/iStockphoto.com; 69: © badmanproduction/iStockphoto.com; 71: © ajafoto/iStockphoto.com; 72: © ALLEKO/iStockphoto.com; 78, 79: © TheCrimsonMonkey/iStockphoto.com; 80: © cpjanes/iStockphoto.com; 83: © robynmac/iStockphoto.com; 90: © svari-ophoto/iStockphoto.com; 93: © burwellphotography/iStockphoto.com; 102, 103: © Paul_Brighton/iStockphoto.com; 104: © Robert Ingelhart/iStockphoto.com; 112, 115: © Tanya_F/iStockphoto.com; 117: © HoangPhoto/iStockphoto.com; 118: © Andrea Mink/iStockphoto.com; 125: © natalisla/iStockphoto.com

The Countryman Press
www.countrymanpress.com

A division of W. W. Norton & Company, Inc.
500 Fifth Avenue, New York, NY 10110
www.wwnorton.com

For information about special discounts for bulk purchases, please contact
W. W. Norton Special Sales at specialsales@wwnorton.com or 800-233-4830.

Printed in the United States

Library of Congress Cataloging-in-Publication Data

Sweeney, Monica.
Best dips & apps ever : fun and easy spreads, snacks, and savory bites / Monica Sweeney.
    pages cm
Includes index.
ISBN 978-1-58157-323-7 (pbk.)
1. Dips (Appetizers) 2. Appetizers. I. Title. II. Title: Best dips and apps ever.

TX740.S94 2015
641.81'2—dc23

                    2015018293

10 9 8 7 6 5 4 3 2 1

TO SARAH SWEENEY,
FOR WORDS OF WISDOM AND TACOS.

BEST DIPS & APPS EVER
CONTENTS

Chapter Five: Fresh Veggies and Seaside Snacks / 103

Introduction

Whether you are hosting a party, attending a potluck, or are just trying to put food on the table, it can be easy to fall into a tired routine of cooking the same thing time and again. Sometimes a home cook needs a little more inspiration than riffling through the recipe box.

The selection of recipes in this book offers a little bit of everything. You will discover with every page turn that these dishes will take your cooking from winter and autumn, with warming comfort foods that make every scrumptious bite feel like home, to spring and summer, with savory treats and hors d'oeuvres made with crisp fresh vegetables and zesty spices, perfect for a picnic or backyard gathering. Whatever the season, you're sure to find new ideas to perk up your menu.

Fit for the seasoned home cook and the hesitant newbie, some of these recipes require a little extra time and affection, while others are incredibly quick and easy to throw together in a time crunch. No matter what skill level you are starting from, your new dishes will impress family and friends, making your home the best restaurant in town!

CHAPTER ONE
DIPS

Classic Hummus

There are few comforts greater than hummus with pita chips and veggies. Just a quick spin in the food processor and this snack can be yours! A healthy dip with endless potential, try tossing a handful of roasted red peppers or a seeded jalapeño in with the base ingredients to amplify the flavor power of this crudité staple.

Yield: about 2½ cups

2 cups canned chickpeas, drained

3 garlic cloves, peeled and minced

⅓ cup tahini sesame paste

Juice of 2 lemons

1½ tablespoons salt

2 tablespoons water

Pinch of paprika

1 teaspoon extra-virgin olive oil

Combine all ingredients except the paprika and olive oil into a food processor. Mix until pureed, stopping once or twice to scrape the sides and reincorporate with the mixture. Sprinkle with paprika and a dash of olive oil upon serving.

"At a dinner party one should eat wisely but not too well, and talk well but not too wisely."
—W. Somerset Maugham

Guacamole

Avocados may be the closest thing to produce perfection. This recipe puts its focus on the delicious, fresh, and flavor-packed ingredients like tangy lime, fiery jalapeños, and zesty cilantro that make guacamole taste so great. It will be sure to please as a stand-alone dip with corn chips, but this guacamole can play a leading role in other recipes, from omelets to hearty sandwiches.

Yield: 2 servings

Juice of 1 lime

3 avocados, peeled and halved

½ teaspoon salt

½ teaspoon ground cumin

½ teaspoon cayenne pepper

½ medium onion, diced

½ jalapeño pepper, seeded and minced

2 Roma tomatoes, seeded and diced

1 tablespoon chopped cilantro

1 clove garlic, minced

Set aside 1 tablespoon of lime juice and add the rest to a bowl with the avocados. Coat evenly, and then add the salt, cumin, and cayenne pepper. Mash with a fork or potato masher until blended. Fold in the remaining ingredients, including the lime juice, until mixed evenly. Serve at room temperature.

Cheesy Garlic Artichoke Dip

This hot and tasty dip is packed with delicious garlic flavor and just the right amount of artichokes to add taste and texture. Served with pita bread, chips, or raw vegetables, this dip ranks high on the list of best comfort foods.

Yield: 3 cups

1 head garlic

2 tablespoons extra-virgin olive oil

1 12-ounce jar artichoke hearts, drained

4 ounces cream cheese

½ cup sour cream or yogurt

¼ cup mayonnaise

¼ cup green onion, chopped

½ teaspoon freshly ground black pepper

1½ cups shredded cheese

Preheat the oven to 425°F. Slice off the top of a head of garlic, exposing the cloves inside. Place in foil and drizzle the olive oil over the garlic. Close the top of the foil over the head of garlic and place on a baking sheet. Cook for 30 minutes. Remove from the oven and let cool. Peel the outside skin of the garlic and remove the cloves. Reduce the oven temperature to 350°F. In a bowl, crush the garlic cloves into a paste. Chop the artichoke hearts into small chunks. In a large bowl, mix all ingredients together, reserving ½ cup of shredded cheese. Scoop the mixture into a baking dish and sprinkle the top with the remaining cheese. Bake for 35 minutes, broiling in the last 3 to 5 minutes to brown the top.

Cauliflower-Curry Dip

Cauliflower is always the last to go on the crudité platter, so use it for this dip instead! This cauliflower puree shares many great qualities with hummus, but this recipe takes a turn and adds the deep flavor of curry.

Yield: 2–4 servings

1 head cauliflower

½ cup water

2 tablespoons unsalted butter, softened

2 teaspoons curry powder

2 cloves garlic, minced

1 teaspoon lemon juice

Pinch of salt and freshly ground pepper

Break cauliflower into small florets, halving them lengthwise. Slice the larger stems and core into chunks. In a medium saucepan, bring the water to a boil over medium heat. Cook the cauliflower pieces, covered, for about 5 minutes or until tender. Strain the cauliflower, reserving the water. Add cauliflower, ¼ cup cooking water, butter, curry powder, garlic, lemon juice, salt, and pepper into a food processor and pulse until smoothly blended. Transfer to a serving bowl and lightly sprinkle with curry.

"Training is everything. The peach was once a bitter almond; cauliflower is nothing but cabbage with a college education."

—Mark Twain

Baked Fontina Cheese Dip

Not quite a fondue, this savory cheese dip is equally rich in flavor and best when piping hot. The rosemary and garlic enhance the great blend of Parmesan and Fontina, and taste incredible on a toasted baguette or with fresh vegetables.

Yield: 4–6 servings

1½ pounds Fontina cheese

¼ cup Parmesan cheese

¼ cup olive oil

5 cloves garlic, minced

1 tablespoon fresh thyme, minced

1 teaspoon fresh rosemary, minced

½ teaspoon dried basil

Pinch of salt and freshly ground black pepper

Preheat the broiler on high. Arrange the cheese in a 12-inch cast-iron pan and drizzle with olive oil. Combine the garlic, thyme, rosemary, and basil and sprinkle evenly over the cheese. Broil for 5 to 6 minutes or until the cheese is bubbling. Add salt and pepper to taste. Serve immediately with sliced baguette or vegetables.

"Cheese: milk's leap toward immortality."

—Clifton Fadiman

Adobo Salsa

This blend of fresh vegetables and hot peppers makes one fiery salsa. For those who prefer a little less spice, swap some of the hot peppers for sweet fruit like mango or pineapple.

Yield: 6–8 servings

1 14-ounce can fire-roasted tomatoes

1 cup fresh cherry tomatoes, sliced in half

½ cup white onion, chopped

2 cloves garlic, chopped

½ jalapeño, chopped and seeded

¼ cup chopped red onion

2 chipotle peppers in adobo

1 teaspoon adobo sauce

Pinch of salt and freshly ground black pepper

½ cup cilantro

Juice of 1 lime

Combine all of the ingredients in a food processor or high-powered blender and pulse until chunky.

Avocado Dip

Not your typical guacamole, this avocado dip is smooth like a veggie dip, but with the cool flavor of avocado. The best part about this dip is that it can be complemented by pita bread and fresh vegetables, but it can also be used as a refreshing spread for sandwiches and burgers.

Yield: 1 cup

1 clove garlic

2 tablespoons fresh tarragon

¼ cup lemon zest

2 large avocados

½ cup plain sour cream

½ teaspoon salt

Mince garlic and tarragon in a food processor. Scrape the mixture down and add remaining ingredients. Pulse until smooth.

Tangy Ginger Sriracha

Sriracha, amplified. This five-alarm hot sauce is lacking in spice, but with a few ingredients like zesty ginger and sugary honey, you will have a new favorite dipping go-to sauce.

Yield: 1 cup

6 tablespoons ketchup

2 tablespoon Sriracha

8 teaspoons rice vinegar

4 teaspoons honey

2 teaspoon grated peeled fresh ginger

Combine all ingredients in a bowl and serve with your favorite tortilla chips.

Spinach & Bacon Dip

This hot and cheesy dip is more than just your typical spinach dip. With added bacon and spicy jalapeños, this is fondue turned fiery. Use it as a dip for chips, soft French bread, and vegetables for a savory snack that is sure to be a crowd-pleaser.

Yield: 8–10 servings

1 package fresh baby spinach

16 ounces Velveeta, cut into cubes

4 ounces cream cheese, softened

1 can diced tomatoes, drained

1 jalapeño

8 slices cooked bacon, broken into bits

Combine all of the ingredients into a microwaveable bowl. Microwave on high for 5 minutes or until cheese blend is completely melted. Stop halfway through to stir.

"Life is too short for self-hatred and celery sticks."

—Marilyn Wann

Pomegranate Cheese Dip

Imagine the sweet and savory combination of baked brie and jam, and then imagine it in the form of pomegranates blended with a smooth, cheesy dip. The fruit adds just the right amount of sweet to this cheesy concoction, and a hint of citrus makes this dip even more special.

Yield: 2 cups

½ cup cream cheese, softened

1 cup goat cheese

Pinch of salt and freshly ground black pepper

3 tablespoons fresh chives, sliced

¼ cup fresh parsley, chopped

2 teaspoons lemon zest

¾ cup pomegranate seeds

Blend cream cheese, goat cheese, salt, and pepper together in a bowl. Fold in the remaining ingredients, adding the pomegranate seeds last.

CHAPTER TWO

BITE-SIZED TREATS

Savory Sausage Puffs

These delicious pastries are hard to put down. The best part of this recipe is that you can feel free to be creative with the variety of sausages you choose for each batch. Whether it's a sweet chicken-apple sausage or a spicy pork sausage, these sausage rolls bring out bold flavors with every bite.

Yield: 6–8 servings

¼ teaspoon dried basil

¼ teaspoon dried oregano

½ pound sausage, removed from casing

1 sheet pre-made puff pastry

Preheat the oven to 400°F. Mix sausage and spices. Unroll the puff pastry onto a floured surface. Using a pizza cutter, slice the pastry into three even sections. Roll out long tubes of sausage to fit the length of each section of puff pastry. Fold the puff pastry neatly over the sausage, pressing to seal the edges. Using a pizza cutter, slice the pastry tubes into 1-inch (bite-sized) portions and place them open-face down on a baking sheet. Bake for 15 minutes or until cooked through.

"Humor keeps us alive. Humor and food. Don't forget food. You can go a week without laughing."
—Joss Whedon

Crab Rangoons

Happiness is crabmeat wrapped in a fried pastry. This recipe is forgiving, and the ratio of crabmeat to cream cheese can be adjusted based on your preferences for one or the other. For the seafood lover, you can never go wrong with adding more crab.

Yield: 25 crab Rangoons

⅛ cup sour cream

1 8-ounce package cream cheese

2 teaspoons soy sauce

1 teaspoon sugar

¼ teaspoon Chinese five-spice

1 clove garlic, minced

1 green onion, sliced

1 teaspoon ginger, minced

1 cup crabmeat

25 wonton wrappers

In a large bowl, blend the sour cream, cream cheese, soy sauce, sugar, and Chinese five-spice together until smooth. Fold in the garlic, green onion, ginger, and crabmeat to make the filling. Lay out the wonton wrappers and drop 1 to 2 tablespoons of filling on the center of each. Using your fingers, dampen the edges of the wonton wrappers with water. Pinch the edges together to seal the filling inside. In a nonstick pan, heat 1½ to 2 inches of oil to medium high. Cook 4 to 6 of the crab Rangoons at a time until they are golden brown. Remove the Rangoons from the oil with tongs or a slotted spoon. Place them on a plate or cooling rack lined with paper towels to soak up the excess oil prior to serving.

Spicy Fried Pickles

There are two fried pickle camps: spears or slices. From where I'm standing, slices reign supreme because of the great balance of hot pickle to flaky crust. Whichever way you choose to fry them up, these are by far the best bar snack that you can bring home.

Yield: 6–8 servings

4 cups vegetable oil

⅓ cup yellow cornmeal

⅔ cup all-purpose flour

2 teaspoons garlic powder

3 teaspoons paprika

1 teaspoon cayenne pepper

½ teaspoon cumin

1 16-ounce jar of dill pickles, drained and patted dry

½ cup banana peppers

Heat oil to 375°F in a deep stock pot. On a plate or in a shallow bowl, mix together the dry ingredients until evenly blended. Coat the pickles and peppers in the mixture until covered completely. Using a spider strainer or metal tongs, carefully lower 10 to 15 of the pickles and peppers into the hot oil. Let cook for 2 to 3 minutes or until golden brown. Remove the pickles and peppers using the spider strainer or metal tongs. Place them on a cooling rack or plate lined with paper towels to soak up the excess oil prior to serving.

"One cannot have too large a party."

—Jane Austen

Stuffed Mushrooms

Mushrooms stuffed with buttery breadcrumbs are nothing short of perfection. This particular recipe is vegetarian, but carnivores may want to add crunchy bacon to the tops of each mushroom for an extra element of flavor.

Yield: 10–12 servings

3 (8-ounce) packages button mushrooms

1 stick butter

½ cup Italian breadcrumbs

¼ teaspoon ground rosemary

Pinch of salt and freshly ground pepper

1 tablespoon green onion, chopped

Juice and zest of 1 lemon

Wash the mushrooms and remove the stems. Set 10 stems aside and discard the rest. Let the mushrooms dry for a couple of hours or overnight. Preheat the oven to 400°F. Melt the butter and chop up the mushroom stems. Combine breadcrumbs, rosemary, salt, pepper, and green onion in a bowl until blended. Add 1 tablespoon of lemon juice. Add more breadcrumbs if the mixture is too wet. Arrange the mushroom caps cavity-side up on a baking sheet. Spoon the mixture into the caps until full. Cook for 40 minutes.

Honeydew & Prosciutto

The underappreciated member of the melon family, honeydew takes center stage in this spin on the traditional cantaloupe wrapped in prosciutto recipe. The blend of juicy, fresh fruit and savory prosciutto will become the new standard.

Yield: 20–25 honeydew balls

1 honeydew melon

12 slices prosciutto

Slice the honeydew in half, removing the seeds. Using a melon baller, firmly press into the flesh of the melon and twist to form ball shape. Continue forming melon balls until the melon has been cleaned. Tear prosciutto into manageable pieces and wrap around the melon balls. Place seam-facedown on serving platter or secure with toothpicks.

"One cannot think well, love well, sleep well, if one has not dined well."
—Virginia Woolf

Cucumbers & Tomatoes

These bite-sized appetizers bring raw vegetables and dip to a new playing field. The refreshing cucumber and creamy dill spread are just the right size, and the sun-dried tomatoes bring in bold flavor.

Yield: 15–20 slices

1 (8-ounce) package cream cheese, softened

1 teaspoon dried dill weed

1 teaspoon dried tarragon

¼ cup mayonnaise

½ teaspoon garlic powder

Pinch of salt and freshly ground black pepper

1 cucumber, sliced

12 sun-dried tomatoes

Blend the cream cheese, dill, tarragon, mayo, garlic powder, salt, and pepper in a food processor until smooth. Pour mixture into a pastry bag and pipe onto cucumber slices. Top with sun-dried tomatoes.

Fried Artichokes

Crunchy on the outside and hot and tangy on the inside, these artichokes take just minutes and are endlessly delicious. Cut the artichoke hearts in half if you prefer small, bite-sized pieces. Serve with your favorite dipping sauce like a marinara or chipotle mayo.

Yield: 4 servings

4 cups olive oil

½ cup flour

1 tablespoon garlic salt

1 teaspoon freshly ground black pepper

1 egg, beaten with 1 tablespoon water for egg wash

1 jar artichoke hearts, drained

Parsley, for garnish

Heat olive oil in medium saucepan to 375°F. Mix flour, garlic salt, and pepper in a bowl. Dip artichokes in egg wash and then dredge in the flour mixture. Fry for 2 minutes or until golden brown. Remove artichokes from the oil and set on a cooling rack or plate lined with paper towels to soak up excess oil. Sprinkle with parsley and serve with dipping sauce.

Fried Ravioli

If traditional ravioli weren't good enough, this fried ravioli recipe will be the extra flavor boost you need. The best part of this recipe is that it doesn't limit the style of filling that you can use. Try it out with any style, from mushroom, lobster, or traditional cheese ravioli to butternut-squash ravioli.

Yield: 4–6 servings

Olive oil

1 cup buttermilk

2 cups bread crumbs

Pinch of salt and freshly ground black pepper

1 tablespoon oregano

1 box or 25 fresh ravioli

¼ cup freshly grated Parmesan

1 cup marinara sauce of your choice

In a large frying pan, heat 2 inches of olive oil over medium heat to 325°F. Pour the buttermilk into one bowl and the bread crumbs, salt, pepper, and oregano into another. Dunk the ravioli in the buttermilk first and then dredge in the breadcrumb mixture. Arrange coated ravioli onto a baking sheet. Fry the ravioli in small batches for 2 to 3 minutes or until lightly browned. Remove cooked ravioli from the oil and set on a cooling rack or plate lined with paper towels to soak up excess oil. Sprinkle with Parmesan and serve with marinara.

Spinach Pouches

This recipe meets somewhere in between spinach and artichoke dip and Greek spanakopita. For added effect, use fresh chives to tie off the pouches.

Yield: 30 pouches

1 cup canned artichoke hearts, drained and chopped

Pinch of salt and freshly ground black pepper

2 cloves garlic, minced

3 tablespoons shallots, minced

3 tablespoons fresh chives, chopped

1 cup baby spinach, chopped

½ teaspoon dried basil

2 tablespoons cream cheese

½ cup shredded Parmesan cheese

½ cup mozzarella

1 egg, beaten with 1 tablespoon water for egg wash

30 small wonton wrappers

Olive oil

In a food processor, mix the artichoke hearts, salt, and pepper for about 10 seconds. Scoop blended artichokes out and into a mixing bowl. Fold in the garlic, shallots, chives, spinach, basil, cream cheese, Parmesan, and mozzarella until well blended. Brush wonton wrappers with egg wash. Scoop heaping tablespoons of the artichoke filling onto the wontons. With dampened fingers, secure the wrappers around the filling to look like a change purse and twist. In a nonstick pan, heat 2 inches of oil on medium high. Cook 4 to 6 of the pouches at a time until they are golden brown, about 2 to 3 minutes. Remove the purses from the oil with tongs or a slotted spoon. Place them on a cooling rack or plate lined with paper towels to soak up the excess oil prior to serving.

"A good cook is like a sorceress who dispenses happiness."

—Elsa Schiaparelli

Crispy Onion Bhajis

This savory treat is as mouthwatering as classic American onion rings, but is enhanced with a punch of delicious Indian spices. Great as a tasty late-night snack or even as a burger topper, these hot and crunchy onion bhajis bring standard fried onions to a whole new place.

Yield: 4 servings

3 cups vegetable oil

1 cup chickpea flour

1 teaspoon baking powder

2 tablespoons rice flour

1 teaspoon turmeric

½ teaspoon chili powder

½ teaspoon cumin

½ teaspoon coriander

Pinch of salt

½ cup water

2 large onions, thinly sliced

Heat vegetable oil in a saucepan on medium-high heat. In a large bowl, combine the chickpea flour, baking powder, rice flour, turmeric, chili powder, cumin, coriander, salt, and water. Whisk until the batter is smooth. Coat the onions in the batter and drop spoonfuls into the heated oil for 1 to 2 minutes or until golden brown. Fry in batches so the bhaji do not clump and the oil stays evenly heated. Remove cooked bhaji from the oil and set on a cooling rack or plate lined with paper towels to soak up excess oil. Sprinkle with salt and serve immediately.

CHAPTER THREE

BREADS, PIZZAS, AND HAND PIES

Spinach Tart

More than a pizza, this delicious snack combines the incredible flavors of caramelized onions, fresh greens, and cheese over a buttery pastry crust. It can be put together in no time, and offers incredible flavors for even the pickiest eaters.

Yield: 4 servings

1 puff pastry sheet

1 tablespoon olive oil

¼ cup fresh spinach

¼ cup Swiss chard

½ cup of caramelized onion

2 tablespoons fresh basil, chopped

1 medium-sized tomato, thinly sliced

½ cup shredded mozzarella cheese

¼ cup shredded Parmesan cheese

Preheat the oven to 400°F. Unroll the puff pastry onto a floured surface. Fold the edges of the pastry to form a ½-inch crust. Brush the puff pastry with olive oil and bake in the oven for 10 minutes. Remove from the oven and add the spinach, Swiss chard, caramelized onion, basil, sliced tomato, and sprinkle on the cheeses. Bake for another 10 minutes or so, or until the crust has browned and the cheese is bubbling.

"Before we begin our banquet, I would like to say a few words. And here they are: *Nitwit! Blubber! Oddment! Tweak!* Thank you."

—Albus Dumbledore

Mini Margherita Pizzas

A little something for everyone! These mini pizzas are great for large groups and incredibly simple to put together. The traditional Margherita never fails, but additional ingredients like bacon or prosciutto can add an extra layer of flavor to this great snack.

Yield: 15–20 mini pizzas

One 12-inch thin-crust pizza crust

½ cup marinara sauce

6 ounces fresh mozzarella cheese, sliced

2 Roma tomatoes, thinly sliced

1 tablespoon crushed red pepper

6–8 fresh basil leaves

1 tablespoon Parmesan, powdered

Preheat oven to 450°F. Using a 2-inch metal cookie cutter, press out 15 to 20 circles from pizza crust. If you do not have a cookie cutter, slice crust into squares with a pizza cutter or knife. Arrange mini pizza crusts onto a foil-lined baking sheet. Top with marinara sauce, sliced mozzarella, and sliced tomatoes. Bake for 8 to 10 minutes or until cheese is bubbling. Finish with crushed red pepper, fresh basil, and a sprinkle of Parmesan.

Chicken Empanadas

The father of all hand pies, the chicken empanada has just the right amount of spice and is endlessly satisfying. Incredible on their own, these empanadas will be an instant crowd-pleaser with the addition of Oaxaca cheese or a spicy chipotle mayo.

Yield: 6–8 servings

1 cup chicken, cooked and shredded

½ cup cheddar cheese, grated

½ cup Monterey jack cheese, grated

3 tablespoons green onions, minced

1 can green chili, chopped

1 teaspoon minced garlic

½ teaspoon dried cilantro

½ teaspoon cumin, ground

½ teaspoon paprika

Pinch of salt and freshly ground black pepper

2 sheets pie pastry

3 egg yolks

2 tablespoons kosher salt

1 tablespoon chili powder

Preheat the oven to 400°F. In a bowl, combine the chicken, cheeses, green onions, green chili, garlic, cilantro, spices, salt, and pepper. Unroll the pie pastry onto a lightly floured surface. Using a 4-inch cookie cutter or overturned glass, cut out pastry circles until all of the dough has been used. Spoon 2 tablespoons of the combined ingredients onto the center of the pie pastries. Fold the pie pastry neatly over the meat, pressing to seal the edges.

Crimp with fork if desired. Arrange the empanadas evenly on a baking sheet. Brush with egg yolks, then sprinkle with a mixture of the salt and chili powder. Bake for 12 to 14 minutes or until golden brown.

"My doctor told me I had to stop having intimate dinners for four unless there are three other people."   —Orson Welles

Scallion Pancakes

There's no need to order out when you can make these incredible scallion pancakes at home. Perhaps best served as a late-night snack when a dinner party is winding down, these savory treats are worth the time in preparing the dough.

Yield: 3 pancakes

2 cups all-purpose flour

1 cup boiling water, divided

¼ cup sesame oil

2 cups scallions, thinly sliced

¼ cup vegetable oil

Pinch of salt

Add flour to food processor. Run the processor, slowly adding ¾ cup of boiling water. Mix for 15 seconds or until blended smoothly. On a lightly floured surface, knead the dough into a ball. Place the ball into a bowl and let rest, covered, at room temperature for 30 minutes or refrigerate overnight. Cut the dough into four evenly sized pieces and roll them into balls. Roll out the dough into four circles about 8 inches across. Brush a thin layer of the sesame oil on top of a pancake and then roll it up, jellyroll style. Twist the jellyroll into a spiral, tucking in the ends. Flatten and shape back into a circle. Repeat the last three steps, but this time add the scallions to each pancake before rolling. Do this for each pancake. Heat oil at medium-high heat in a nonstick pan. Once simmering, carefully place the pancake into the oil. Cook each side for about 2 minutes, or until golden brown. Place pancake onto a cooling rack or plate lined with paper towels to soak up the excess oil. Cook the remaining pancakes, slice into wedges, and serve with the Scallion Pancake Soy Sauce, on page 124.

Herbed Naan

With crunchy bubbles on the outside and a soft and chewy inside, this pillowy flat-bread is flawless. Typically perfected in a tandoor oven, this North Indian bread can also be made at home in the oven, so that warm, elastic bread is not too far away.

Yield: 8 pieces

2½ teaspoons dry yeast

2 tablespoons sugar

1 cup warm water, divided

4½ cups all-purpose flour

1 teaspoon baking powder

¼ teaspoon ground coriander

2 teaspoons salt

2 tablespoons plain Greek yogurt

3 tablespoons milk

1 large egg, lightly beaten

2 tablespoons vegetable oil

3 tablespoons unsalted butter, melted

1 cup fresh herbs, toasted

Combine yeast, sugar, and ¼ cup warm water in a bowl and let stand for 5 to 10 minutes, or until foamy. Mix flour, baking powder, coriander, and salt. Add yeast mixture, yogurt, milk, eggs, vegetable oil, and remaining water. Knead the dough, adding flour as necessary to keep it from getting sticky, for several minutes or until elastic. (This can be done by hand or in a food processor or mixer.) Place dough into a large bowl that has been lightly coated with oil. Cover and let rise until doubled, about 1 to 1½ hours. Punch down the dough and separate into 8 pieces. Roll the dough into balls and lay out on a lightly floured surface. Cover with a damp kitchen towel and let rise for 40 to 60 minutes or until doubled. Place a pizza stone in the oven and preheat to 450°F.

On a lightly floured surface, roll out dough to about 6 to 8 inches in diameter. Turn on the broiler and place 2 pieces of dough on the pizza stone. Let cook for 2 to 4 minutes, or until the tops bubble slightly. Repeat with the remaining dough. Brush the tops of the bread with melted butter. Sprinkle with toasted herbs of your choice.

"One of the very nicest things about life is the way we must regularly stop whatever it is we are doing and devote our attention to eating. "
—Luciano Pavarotti and William Wright

Sesame Breadsticks

When hunger pangs strike, reach for the breadsticks. These crunchy spears are coated with sesame seeds for an extra element of texture and are great on their own or paired with an Italian dinner.

Yield: 15–18 breadsticks

1 cup warm water, divided

1 teaspoon honey

1 envelope active dry yeast

1½ cups bread flour

1½ cups all-purpose flour

1 teaspoon sugar

1 teaspoon salt

2 tablespoons sesame oil

Cornmeal for sprinkling

1 egg, beaten with 1 tablespoon water for egg wash

¼ cup sesame seeds, toasted

Prepare a ¼ cup of warm water and stir in honey. Add the yeast and let rest for 5 to 10 minutes or until foamy. In a large bowl, mix together the flours, sugar, and salt. Add the yeast mixture, sesame oil, and remaining warm water and stir together. On a lightly floured surface, knead the dough for about 10 minutes or until smooth. Place the dough in a lightly greased bowl and cover with a damp towel. Let rise until doubled, about 1 hour. Press down the dough and allow to rest for another 5 minutes. Roll out the dough on a lightly floured surface. Shape into a large rectangle. Using a pizza cutter, slice the dough into long strips about 1 inch wide. Arrange the breadsticks onto baking sheets sprinkled with cornmeal. Brush with egg wash and sprinkle

with sesame seeds. Cover with a damp towel and let rise for another hour. While the dough is rising, preheat the oven to 425°F. Bake for 15 minutes or until crunchy.

Savory Pinwheels

These little pastries are fun additions to any gathering. With such great elements as goat cheese, spinach, bacon, herbs, and spices, these buttery pinwheels will be an instant favorite.

Yield: 6–8 servings

1 sheet puff pastry

5 ounces goat cheese

⅛ teaspoon garlic powder

Pinch of salt and freshly ground black pepper

¼ cup green onions, chopped

5 slices bacon, crisp and broken into pieces

1½ cups fresh spinach, chopped

Preheat the oven to 350°F. Unroll the pastry dough and divide into 2 long rectangles. Spread the goat cheese onto the dough and then top with garlic powder, salt, pepper, green onions, bacon, and spinach. Roll the dough up like a jellyroll, pressing the edges together at the end to seal. Divide the roll into 6 to 8 slices and arrange the slices evenly onto an ungreased cookie sheet. Do this for both rectangles. Bake for 15 minutes or until the dough is golden brown.

"If you really want to make a friend, go to someone's house and eat with him . . . the people who give you their food give you their heart."

—Cesar Chavez

Cheesy Puff Pastries

With a focal point of Gruyere and Parmesan cheeses, this recipe is nothing short of heavenly. Savory, cheesy, and a little bit salty, these bite-sized pastries can be addicting.

Yield: 40 puffs

½ cup milk

½ cup light cream

1 stick unsalted butter

½ teaspoon garlic powder

1 teaspoon salt

Pinch of freshly ground black pepper

½ teaspoon nutmeg

1 cup all-purpose flour

4 large eggs

¼ cup freshly grated Parmesan

½ cup grated Gruyere

1 egg, beaten with 1 tablespoon water for egg wash

Preheat the oven to 425°F. Heat the milk, cream, butter, garlic powder, salt, pepper, and nutmeg over medium heat in a saucepan until boiling. Add all of the flour and beat rapidly until blended. Reduce the heat to low and cook for another 2 minutes, stirring constantly. Pour the hot liquid into a food processor with a steel blade, adding the 4 eggs and both cheeses. Pulse until the mixture has thickened and is free of clumps. Pour the mixture into a pastry bag with a large round tip and pipe evenly into small mounds on parchment-lined baking sheets. Brush each pastry lightly with egg wash and finish with a sprinkle of Gruyere cheese. Bake for 15 minutes or until golden brown.

Prosciutto Pizza

With a crispy thin crust, peppery arugula, and freshly sliced prosciutto, this healthier-style pizza is packed with flavor. To serve as appetizers for a gathering, slice the pizza into small squares rather than traditional wedges for the perfect-sized finger food.

Yield: 2–3 servings

Thin crust pizza dough

Cornmeal for sprinkling

Olive oil for brushing

½ cup marinara sauce

6 ounces arugula

2 teaspoons extra-virgin olive oil

1 teaspoon red wine vinegar

½ teaspoon dried oregano

Pinch of salt and freshly ground black pepper

4–5 pieces thinly sliced prosciutto

1 ounce Parmesan cheese, shaved

Preheat the oven and stone to 550°F. Roll out pizza dough into a 10-inch round on a lightly floured surface. If the dough starts to shrink, let sit for 5 minutes and then continue rolling. When the dough is ready, sprinkle cornmeal onto a baking sheet lined with parchment paper. Lightly brush the dough with olive oil. Spread the marinara sauce onto the pizza evenly, leaving a half-inch border for the crust. Carefully slide the pizza onto the stone from the baking sheet. Bake for 10 minutes or until golden brown. Toss the arugula, olive oil, vinegar, oregano, salt, and pepper in a bowl and distribute evenly across the pizza. Shred the prosciutto into pieces and scatter evenly. Top with Parmesan.

Beef & Lamb
Samosas

These little hand pies are full of flavor and spice. For those who prefer chicken, replace the beef and lamb with ⅔ pound lean ground chicken for another great version of the samosa.

Yield: 6–8 servings

2 tablespoons olive oil

⅓ pound ground beef

⅓ pound ground lamb

½ cup yellow onion, chopped

½ cup peas, fresh or thawed

½ cup carrots, diced

½ teaspoon ground cumin

¼ teaspoon garam masala

¼ teaspoon turmeric

½ teaspoon garlic powder

Pinch of salt and freshly ground black pepper

¼ cup water

1 sheet of puff pastry

1 egg, beaten with 1 tablespoon water for egg wash

Preheat oven to 400°F. In a medium skillet, heat 1 tablespoon olive oil over medium heat. Add the ground beef and lamb and break into small pieces. Remove from the heat and strain out the grease. Safely discard the hot grease. In the same skillet, heat remaining olive oil over medium heat. Cook the onion, peas, and carrots for 2 to 3 minutes. Stir in the meat, adding the cumin, garam masala, turmeric, garlic powder, salt, pepper, and water. Continue to cook for 3 to 4 more minutes or until the water has evaporated.

Remove from the heat. Roll out the puff pastry and divide into squares. Drop 2 tablespoons of the meat mixture in the center of the squares. Fold the pastry over the filling and pinch the edges to seal the samosas. Brush the samosas with egg wash and arrange on a greased baking sheet. Bake for 12 to 15 minutes or until lightly browned.

CHAPTER FOUR

HEARTY EATS

Classic Chicken Wings

From meat-and-potatoes lovers to refined foodies, chicken wings are the appetizer go-to loved by all. This classic marinade is as easy to make as it is delicious. Whether you're preparing for a tailgate party or just have a craving for some good old-fashioned wings, this simple recipe will have everyone in your crowd raving.

Yield: 6–8 servings

2 tablespoons all-purpose flour

1 teaspoon salt

¼ teaspoon pepper

¼ teaspoon garlic powder

1 tablespoon Old Bay seasoning

2 pounds chicken wingettes and drumettes

2½ tablespoons hot sauce

2 tablespoons unsalted butter, melted

2 tablespoons Worcestershire sauce

Preheat the oven to 500°F. In a bowl, mix the flour, salt, pepper, garlic powder, and Old Bay seasoning. Coat the chicken evenly. Arrange the chicken on a parchment or foil-lined baking sheet without overlapping. Cook for 45 minutes or until crispy, turning the chicken midway through with tongs. While the chicken cooks, whisk the hot sauce, butter, and Worcestershire sauce together. Remove the chicken from the oven and use tongs to dunk the pieces in the sauce, coating evenly.

"And I like large parties. They're so intimate. At small parties there isn't any privacy."

—F. Scott Fitzgerald, *The Great Gatsby*

Lime & Chili Chicken Kebabs

Nothing says summer like lightly charred kebabs fresh off the grill. The spices and citrus add a delightful zing to complement most anything you decide to put on your kebabs, from chicken, pineapple, onion, and peppers, to bites of summer squash and zucchini. This recipe makes putting meat and vegetables on a stick taste like a culinary masterpiece.

Yield: 4 servings

- 3 tablespoons olive oil
- 1½ tablespoons red wine vinegar
- Juice of 1 lime
- ½ teaspoon chili powder
- ½ teaspoon paprika
- ½ teaspoon onion powder
- ½ teaspoon garlic powder
- 1 teaspoon dried cilantro
- 1 teaspoon Sriracha
- 1 teaspoon cayenne pepper
- Pinch of salt and freshly ground black pepper
- 1 pound skinless, boneless chicken thighs

Combine all ingredients except chicken in a mixing bowl and whisk until completely blended. Cut chicken into 1½ inch pieces. Arrange the chicken in a shallow baking dish and coat with sauce. Cover and let marinate in the refrigerator for one hour at minimum. Preheat the grill to medium-high. Lightly grease just before using. Thread chicken onto skewers and grill 10 to 15 minutes or until cooked through. If using wooden skewers, presoak them in water for 20 minutes before using.

Fiery Meatballs

The sauce makes this recipe. Whether you swear by making meatballs from scratch or prefer the ease of the store-bought variety, the delicious blend of smoky spices and savory beef stock bring out the best in this well-loved party staple.

Yield: About 25 meatballs

2 tablespoons salted butter

¼ cup all-purpose flour

1 cup beef broth

¾ cup A1 steak sauce

½ cup chili sauce

½ cup ketchup

2 tablespoons Worcestershire sauce

1 teaspoon hot pepper sauce

1 package or 25 small meatballs

In a large saucepan, melt butter on a medium to high heat. Add flour and stir until light brown to make a roux. Add beef broth and stir until thickened. Add the remaining ingredients, adding the meatballs last. Keep pan covered except to stir occasionally. Cook for 15 to 20 minutes or until heated through.

"I am not a glutton. I am an explorer of food."

—Erma Bombeck

Vegetable Pot Stickers

Fresh and delicious homemade dumplings aren't too far off with this great recipe. Sautéing these dumplings will turn them nice and brown, but you can also steam them for a slightly healthier variety.

Yield: About 24 dumplings

2 tablespoons vegetable oil

1 red onion, sliced

1 tablespoon minced ginger

1 cup sliced shiitake mushrooms

1 cup white cabbage, shredded

1 cup carrots, shredded

2 cloves garlic, minced

¼ teaspoon Chinese five-spice powder

2 tablespoons chives, finely sliced

1 teaspoon sesame oil

1 teaspoon rice wine vinegar

¼ cup chopped cilantro

1 package round dumpling or gyoza skins

¼ cup water

Heat oil in a large sauté pan on medium-high. Cook onions and ginger for 2 minutes or until aromatic. Stir in the mushrooms, cabbage, carrots, garlic, five-spice powder, and chives. When the ingredients have softened, strain in a colander and transfer to a bowl. Drizzle in sesame oil, vinegar, and add cilantro when cool. Lay out the dumpling skins and drop the filling into the center of each. Fold the dough over and pinch edges to seal. Return the

dumplings to a hot pan coated with oil. Cook for 3 to 4 minutes or until the bottoms have browned. Add the water and cover to steam the dumplings. When the water has evaporated, remove from heat. Serve immediately with Tangy Pot Stickers Sauce, on page 125.

Beef Satay

This light ginger marinade makes these beef skewers exceptional. With a little added peanut sauce for dipping, this appetizer is full of flavor and great for any occasion.

Yield: 4 servings

1 tablespoon fresh ginger

1 medium onion

¼ cup rice wine vinegar

4 cloves garlic

2 tablespoons sugar

½ teaspoon ground cumin

2 tablespoons sesame oil

1 cup soy sauce

1 teaspoon chili paste

Juice of 1 lemon

Juice of 1 lime

1½ pounds sirloin

Puree all of the ingredients except sirloin in a mixer until smooth. Prepare the beef by cutting it into long strips. Place the beef in a bowl or baking dish and pour the marinade over, coating the meat evenly. Refrigerate for at least 1 hour or overnight. When ready to cook, preheat the grill or large sauté pan on medium-high. Thread the meat onto the skewers. If using wooden skewers, presoak them in water for 20 minutes before using. Cook the skewers for 2 to 3 minutes on each side, or until they reach the desired doneness. Serve with Peanut Sauce, on page 124.

Spicy Sliders

These sliders are straightforward to make but have tons of flavor. While store-bought sliders are certainly available, mixing up some fresh ground beef and savory ingredients is a simple way to make some of the best tasting juicy burgers around. The slider-style size is fantastic for serving large groups, but this recipe can also go large scale with full-sized burgers.

Yield: 10 sliders

1 pound ground sirloin

1 medium onion, diced

2 tablespoons Worcestershire sauce

1 tablespoon red hot sauce

¼ teaspoon garlic powder

Pinch of salt and freshly ground black pepper

10 small slices cheddar cheese

10 slider buns, toasted

10 small lettuce leaves, any type, for serving

2 Roma or plum tomatoes, thinly sliced crosswise, for serving

Mix ground sirloin with onion, Worcestershire sauce, hot sauce, garlic powder, salt, and pepper. Scoop into small patties (about two tablespoons) and arrange on a parchment-lined baking sheet. Preheat broiler and broil for 4 to 5 minutes. Top burgers with cheese just before removing from the oven. Plate with slider buns, lettuce, tomato, and any additional toppings of your choice.

Beef Lettuce Wraps

These lettuce wraps are a delectable and healthy alternative to many typical appetizers. The blend of ingredients is crunchy and zesty, and the beef can be swapped with other proteins like chicken, shrimp, and even tofu.

Yield: 4 servings

1 teaspoon vegetable oil

1 pound ground beef

2 teaspoons ginger, minced

2 scallions, chopped

2 cloves garlic, minced

2 tablespoons soy sauce

1 teaspoon sesame oil

1 teaspoon red pepper flakes

¼ cup water chestnuts

¼ cup hoisin sauce

¼ cup chopped peanuts

Salt and freshly ground black pepper

1 head Bibb lettuce

Heat oil at medium-high heat in a large sauté pan. Add beef and cook until browned, and then add the ginger, scallions, garlic, soy sauce, sesame oil, red pepper flakes, water chestnuts, and hoisin. Stir for another minute and remove from the heat. Fold in the peanuts and sprinkle with salt and pepper. Scoop spoonfuls into the lettuce and serve immediately.

Cheesy Arancini

Closely tied in deliciousness with traditional Italian meatballs, arancini are flavorful fried balls of rice and cheese that can be enhanced with the addition of meats like ham or prosciutto, or vegetables like tomatoes or peas. Be sure to make enough for everyone, because sharing is no small task.

Yield: 16 arancini

3 cups chicken broth

¼ teaspoon salt

1 cup arborio rice

2 tablespoons pine nuts, toasted

½ cup shredded mozzarella cheese

½ cup shredded Fontina cheese

2 tablespoons fresh parsley, chopped

¼ cup fresh basil, chopped

2 cloves garlic, chopped

2 large eggs

½ cup grated Parmesan cheese

1½ cups breadcrumbs

vegetable oil

In a medium saucepan, heat the broth and salt to a boil over medium-high heat. Add the rice and reduce the heat to a simmer. Cook the rice for 20 minutes or until the broth is absorbed. While the rice is cooking, combine the pine nuts, mozzarella, Fontina, parsley, basil, and garlic in a separate bowl. Scoop the rice onto a parchment-lined baking sheet, spread evenly, and let it cool. Beat the eggs and then gradually stir in the rice, Parmesan, and ⅔ cup of breadcrumbs. Form golf-ball-sized balls with the mixture and make a hole with your finger in the middle of each. Insert 2 teaspoons of the pine nut and cheese mixture. Close up the hole by reshaping the rice ball with your fingers.

Carefully roll the rice balls in the remaining breadcrumbs and arrange onto a parchment-lined baking sheet. Cover the baking sheet and refrigerate for at least 1 hour and at most overnight. In a large saucepan, heat ½ inch vegetable oil to 350°F over medium-high. Carefully add the arancini to the oil and let cook for about 4 minutes, turning to brown each side. Cook them in small batches and place on a cooling rack or plate lined with paper towels to soak up the excess oil. Sprinkle with salt, lightly garnish with parsley, and serve immediately.

"I consider a good dinner party at our house to be where people drink and eat more than they're meant to. My husband is a really fantastic cook. His mother is Italian and if you walk into our house, we assume you're starving."
—Elizabeth Gilbert

Lamb Lollipops

Just big enough to stave off hunger but not so big that they'll take away from the main course, these juicy lamb chops are the perfect appetizer size. Great on the grill or sautéed, the hint of rosemary and garlic adds all the flavor you'll need.

Yield: 6 lamb lollipops

3 tablespoons + 2 tablespoons extra-virgin olive oil, divided

½ cup red wine

1 tablespoon rosemary leaves

1 teaspoon garlic, minced

Pinch of salt and freshly ground black pepper

6 double lamb rib chops (4 ounces each)

2 rosemary sprigs

Preheat the oven to 400°F. Combine 3 tablespoons olive oil, red wine, rosemary, and garlic in a small bowl and set aside. Heat 2 tablespoons of oil in a large, oven-safe sauté pan over medium-high. Sprinkle the lamb with salt and pepper and then lay flat in the pan. Sear the lamb for 2 to 3 minutes, or until the meat has browned. Turn the lamb and cook for another 2 to 3 minutes, basting with the olive oil mixture throughout. Place the sauté pan in the oven and cook for another 5 minutes or until medium-rare. Plate and garnish with fresh rosemary.

"Always remember: If you're alone in the kitchen and you drop the lamb, you can always just pick it up. Who's going to know?"

—Julia Child

Potato Skins

This appetizer is a classic for a reason, perfect for game-day entertaining or as a hearty snack. For an extra kick, top with jalapeños or hot red sauce.

Yield: 8 servings

4 large baking potatoes

3 tablespoons vegetable oil

¼ teaspoon garlic powder

¼ teaspoon paprika

Pinch of salt and freshly ground black pepper

1 tablespoon grated Parmesan cheese

2 cups shredded Cheddar cheese

8 slices bacon, chopped into bits

Clean the potatoes and make perforations using a toothpick. Heat in the microwave for 12 to 14 minutes, stopping halfway through to turn and check for doneness. Once the potatoes have cooled, slice them in half, lengthwise. Scoop out the contents in the middle and discard. Heat 2 inches of vegetable oil in frying pan to 365°F. Mix remaining oil, garlic powder, paprika, salt, pepper, and Parmesan in a small bowl. Brush over skins. Fry the potato skins in batches for 5 minutes. Remove potato skins from the oil and set on a cooling rack or plate lined with paper towels to soak up excess oil. Preheat the oven to 450°F. Arrange potato skins facedown in a greased baking dish. Bake for 8 minutes. Flip the potato skins over and add cheese and bacon. Bake for 8 more minutes or until cheese has melted.

"What I say is that, if a man really likes potatoes, he must be a pretty decent sort of fellow."
—A. A. Milne

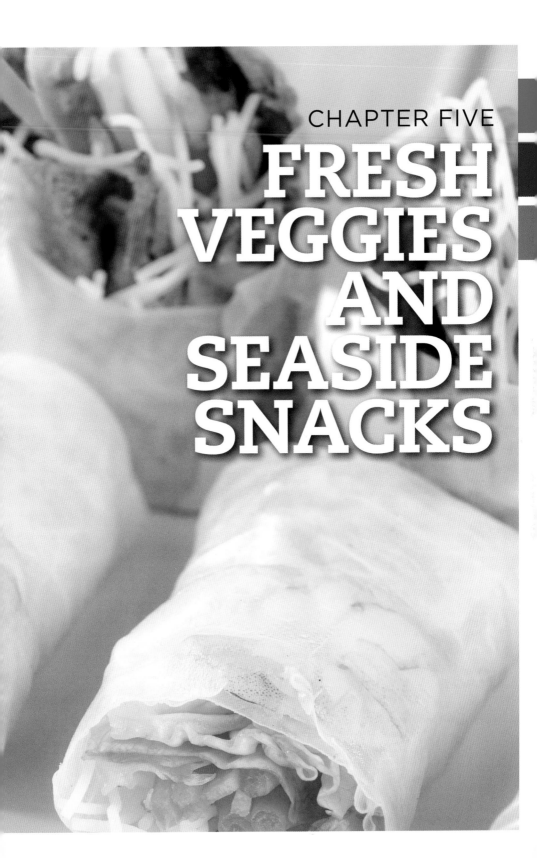

CHAPTER FIVE

FRESH VEGGIES AND SEASIDE SNACKS

Lemon-Ginger Shrimp

This is shrimp cocktail with a personality. A perfect excuse for firing up the grill, lemon-ginger shrimp go great on skewers for kebabs, but are just as delicious plated all on their own. With the zesty flavors of lemon and ginger, these shrimp appetizers have the extra kick you're looking for.

Yield: 6–8 servings

2 teaspoons garlic, peeled and minced

2 tablespoons fresh ginger, minced

3 teaspoons sesame oil

1 tablespoon soy sauce

⅓ cup olive oil

2 tablespoons rice wine vinegar

Pinch of salt and freshly ground black pepper

2 pounds raw jumbo shrimp, peeled

2 tablespoons chives, chopped

Whisk the garlic, ginger, sesame oil, soy sauce, olive oil, rice wine vinegar, salt, and pepper together. Place cleaned shrimp in a bowl or storage container, and pour in the mixture. Cover and let marinate in the refrigerator for 30 minutes. If cooking on skewers, thread the two sides of the shrimp to form a C. Lightly oil the grill or a sauté pan, setting the heat on medium. Cook the shrimp for 2 to 3 minutes per side or until pink. Brush with extra marinade as they cook. Sprinkle with chives and serve.

Swordfish & Vegetable Kebabs

In spring, summer, winter, or fall, there is always an excuse to grill up kebabs. While chicken and steak tend to steal the show, swapping them out for thick-cut pieces of fresh fish like swordfish or salmon offers a delicious and healthy way to fire up the grill at any time of year.

Yield: 4–6 servings

⅓ cup extra-virgin olive oil

2 cloves garlic, minced

1 tablespoon rosemary, finely chopped

½ teaspoon oregano

1 tablespoon lemon zest

Pinch of salt and freshly ground black pepper

1 pound boneless, skinless swordfish steak, cut into chunks

1 zucchini, sliced into thick rounds

1 yellow bell pepper, cut into chunks

1 large red onion, cut into chunks

In a small bowl, combine the olive oil, garlic, rosemary, oregano, lemon zest, salt, and pepper. Toss marinade with swordfish, zucchini, bell peppers, and onion, cover, and let soak in the refrigerator for 30 minutes. Preheat grill on medium-high. Thread the swordfish and vegetables onto the skewers and save the leftover marinade. If using wooden skewers, presoak them in water for 20 minutes before using. Grill the skewers for 5 to 7 minutes, turning gradually, until the salmon and vegetables are cooked and lightly charred. Boil the leftover marinade for 5 minutes and drizzle on top of the skewers when serving.

Panko-Crusted Asparagus

Fresh asparagus is great in almost every form: lightly charred on the grill or sautéed with lemon and butter in a pan; this vegetable has so much potential. One of the best amped-up varieties of asparagus, though, has to be when it is tossed with cheese and breadcrumbs. The combination adds an extra crunch and satisfying cheesiness that will make anyone eager to eat their veggies.

Yield: 4–6 servings

¾ cup panko breadcrumbs

¼ teaspoon oregano

½ teaspoon dried basil

¼ cup Parmesan, grated

Pinch of salt and freshly ground black pepper

1 pound asparagus, trimmed

½ cup flour

2 eggs, lightly beaten

Preheat the oven to 425°F. Combine the breadcrumbs, herbs, Parmesan, salt, and pepper in a bowl. Coat the asparagus in the flour and then dip the asparagus into the eggs. Transfer the coated asparagus into the breadcrumb mixture and cover completely. Arrange the asparagus in one layer on a baking sheet and cook for 10 to 12 minutes, or until golden brown.

"Anyone who's a chef, who loves food, ultimately knows that all that matters is: 'Is it good? Does it give pleasure?'"   —Anthony Bourdain

Crab Cakes

Seafood lovers, unite! In just a few short steps, you can feel like you're on a beach-side boardwalk in no time. These crab cakes are big on flavor, from the fresh pieces of crab to the traditional tartar sauce.

Yield: 6 crab cakes

1 large egg

2½ tablespoons mayonnaise

1½ teaspoons Dijon mustard

1 teaspoon Worcestershire sauce

1 teaspoon Old Bay seasoning

¼ teaspoon salt

¼ cup celery, diced

2 cloves garlic, minced

¼ cup yellow onion, chopped

2 tablespoons fresh parsley, chopped

1 cup crabmeat

½ cup panko breadcrumbs

2 tablespoons vegetable oil for cooking

In a large bowl, combine all of the ingredients except the crabmeat, breadcrumbs, and vegetable oil. Once blended, fold in the crabmeat and the breadcrumbs. Shape the mixture into 6 large crabcakes, cover, and refrigerate for at least 1 hour. In a large saucepan, heat vegetable oil on medium-high. Cook the crabcakes in the saucepan for about 3 to 5 minutes on each side or until golden brown. Place on a cooling rack or plate lined with a paper towel to soak up the excess oil. Top with tartar sauce and serve with lemon wedges.

Roasted Pumpkin-Tomato Bruschetta

Fresh tomatoes, basil, Parmesan, and balsamic on hot, toasted crostini is undoubtedly tasty. Adding pumpkin, however, is a game-changer. This incredible blend of fresh vegetables and sweet roasted pumpkin is sure to be a new favorite.

Yield: Makes 8 slices

½ pumpkin, seeded and rind removed

Salt and freshly ground black pepper

1 baguette

5 tablespoons olive oil, divided

2 tomatoes, diced

2 spring onions, finely chopped

1 tablespoon basil, chopped

2 tablespoons white balsamic reduction

4 ounces Parmesan cheese

Preheat the oven to 375°F. Chop the pumpkin up into ¼ inch cubes and season with salt and pepper. Roast the pumpkin for 30 minutes or until tender. Slice the baguette and arrange the pieces on a baking sheet. Drizzle with 1 tablespoon olive oil and toast for a few minutes until lightly browned. Toss the pumpkin cubes with remaining olive oil, tomatoes, ¼ teaspoon salt, ¼ teaspoon pepper, onions, and basil. Scoop a tablespoon or two of the bruschetta onto the crostini. Drizzle with balsamic reduction and sprinkle with shaved Parmesan.

Potato Pancakes with Salmon & Dill

Whether your family has been making potato pancakes for years or this recipe is new to you, there is no question that potato pancakes are one of the world's most comforting foods. The smoky salmon and crème fraîche build on the great texture of these homemade pancakes.

Yield: Approximately 18–24 pancakes

½ cup crème fraîche

1 teaspoon dill, chopped

1 teaspoon fresh lemon juice

1 pound russet potatoes, peeled (2–3 potatoes)

1 small onion

1 large egg, lightly beaten

3 tablespoons matzo meal

½ teaspoon garlic powder

Pinch of salt and freshly ground black pepper

½ cup vegetable oil

½ pound thinly sliced smoked salmon

¼ cup chives, chopped

Prepare the topping by stirring the crème fraîche, dill, and lemon juice together. Cover and refrigerate until ready to serve. Coarsely shred the potatoes and onion in a food processor. (This can also be done with a box grater.) On a clean, dry kitchen towel, press out any excess moisture from the shredded potatoes and onions. Add the potatoes and onions to a large bowl and stir in the egg, matzo meal, garlic powder, salt, and pepper. Heat the vegetable oil in a large skillet on medium-high. Drop heaping tablespoons of the potatoes onto the pan, flattening them into 3-inch pancakes with a spoon or spatula. You will need to cook in batches. Cook for 3 to 4 minutes on each side, or until the

pancakes have lightly browned. Remove potato pancakes from the oil and set on a cooling rack or plate lined with paper towels to soak up excess oil. Arrange the pancakes on a plate and add a dollop of the crème fraîche mixture to each one. Top with slice of smoked salmon. Garnish with chives.

"Ponder well on this point: the pleasant hours of our life are all connected by a more or less tangible link, with some memory of the table."
—Charles Pierre Monselet

Vietnamese Fresh Rolls

This recipe involves a little bit of extra effort, but with big results. Served chilled, the light rice paper and zesty ingredients of these shrimp rolls are a great alternative to heavier fried spring or egg rolls.

Yield: 16 rolls

1 pound medium shrimp, peeled and deveined

4 ounces rice noodles

16 round rice-paper wrappers

1 cup carrots, shredded

1 bunch mint leaves, pulled from stems

1 bunch basil leaves, pulled from stems

16 small fresh cilantro sprigs

2 Serrano chilies, julienned

1 medium cucumber, julienned

3 medium scallions, diced

8 Bibb lettuce leaves, divided in half

In a medium saucepan, bring water to a boil over medium-high heat. Cook the shrimp for 1 minute or until pink. Strain and cool the shrimp with cold water. Slice the shrimp in half, lengthwise. (Do so by laying the shrimp on a cutting board and slicing horizontally.) Cover the shrimp and refrigerate temporarily. Prepare the rice noodles according to package instructions, drain, and set aside. Fill a large, shallow baking dish with hot water (not boiling). Submerge rice paper in the water for about 15 seconds or until it is soft. Take the rice paper out of the water and lay it gently on a clean, damp towel. Lay the fillings on top of the rice paper, using 2 to 3 pieces of the halved shrimp and

a fingertip full of the remaining ingredients. Do not overfill or the rice paper will break. Fold the bottom half of the rice paper over the filling, and then fold the outsides over. Roll the rest up and arrange on a plate, seam-face down. Serve with the Peanut Sauce from page 124 for dipping.

Smoked Salmon, Cucumber, & Caviar

These delightful little finger sandwiches may just make you want to host afternoon tea. With the smoky flavor of salmon and a bit of caviar, this traditional hors d'oeuvre is simple to make and always appealing.

Yield: 18 pieces

6 slices rye bread

4 ounces cream cheese

1 cucumber, sliced

6 slices smoked salmon

1 cucumber

Fresh dill

1 (3-ounce) can black caviar

Juice of 1 lemon

Spread bread with cream cheese and cut into triangles. Lay cucumber slices on top of cream cheese. Next, layer with a piece of folded salmon. Top with caviar and a sprig of dill. Finish with a squeeze of lemon.

Rhode Island
Stuffies

If you can't be near the beach, bring the beach to you. These stuffed clams are an Ocean State staple, and are best when drizzled with a little bit of hot sauce and a squeeze of lemon before serving.

Yield: 8–10 Stuffies

12 large quahogs, rinsed

¼ cup olive oil

½ stick butter

½ medium onion, minced

1 clove garlic, minced

2 cups dried breadcrumbs

½ teaspoon Old Bay seasoning

¼ teaspoon thyme

3 tablespoons parsley, chopped

¼ red pepper, chopped finely

½ teaspoon dried basil

1 tablespoon lemon juice

½ teaspoon salt

½ teaspoon Tabasco

Preheat oven to 350°F. Fill a deep skillet with ½ inch of water and bring to a boil over medium heat. Add the clams and steam for 4 to 5 minutes or until the shells open. Discard any clams that have not opened. Reserve the cooking liquid and rinse the pan. Scoop out the meat and chop into pieces. Separate the shell halves and clean them out. Heat the olive oil, butter, and onions over medium heat for 2 minutes, or until aromatic. Add in the garlic and cook for another minute. Blend in the breadcrumbs, Old Bay seasoning, thyme,

parsley, red pepper, basil, lemon juice, salt, Tabasco, and ¼ cup cooking water. Stir until the breadcrumbs are moistened throughout, but not too wet. Scoop spoonfuls of the stuffing and fill the clamshells. Place the clamshells on a baking pan and cook for 20 to 25 minutes or until browned at the top.

"You can't just eat good food. You've got to talk about it too. And you've got to talk about it to somebody who understands that kind of food."

–Kurt Vonnegut, *Jailbird*

Cucumber-Lobster Salad

There is nothing like a fresh lobster roll in warm weather. With thinly sliced cucumbers, these tiny lobster wraps are a refreshing take on the original. If lobster is tricky to find, swap it for shrimp or crabmeat for a delightful, summery snack.

Yield: 6–8 servings

1 pound lobster meat

4 teaspoons chives, chopped

1 stalk celery, diced

¼ teaspoon of Old Bay seasoning

2 teaspoons parsley, chopped

1 teaspoon tarragon

⅓ cup mayonnaise

3 tablespoons sour cream

1 teaspoon freshly squeezed lemon juice

½ teaspoon Dijon mustard

Pinch of salt and freshly ground black pepper

1 large cucumber

Toss the lobster, chives, celery, Old Bay, parsley, and tarragon in a mixing bowl. In a separate bowl, mix the mayonnaise, sour cream, lemon juice, and mustard. Fold in the lobster mixture, salt, and pepper until evenly coated. Shave long, wide slices of cucumber using a vegetable peeler. Lay the cucumber slices out and drop a dollop of lobster salad onto one end of each. Starting from the same end, roll the lobster salad into a bundle and secure with a toothpick.

Additional Sauces

Scallion Pancake Soy Sauce

2 tablespoons soy sauce

2 tablespoons rice wine vinegar

¼ teaspoon garlic powder

1 tablespoon finely sliced scallion greens

½ teaspoon grated fresh ginger

2 teaspoons sugar

Tartar Sauce

1 cup mayonnaise

1½ tablespoons sweet pickle relish

1 teaspoon Dijon mustard

1 tablespoon minced red onion

1–2 tablespoons lemon juice, to taste

Salt and freshly ground black pepper, to taste

Peanut Sauce

¾ cup natural-style creamy peanut butter

⅓ cup water

3 tablespoons hoisin sauce

1 tablespoon rice wine vinegar

¼ teaspoon ground ginger

Juice of 1½ limes

4½ teaspoons soy sauce

1 tablespoon granulated sugar

2¼ teaspoons chili-garlic paste

1 medium garlic clove, mashed to a paste

½ teaspoon toasted sesame oil

Tangy Pot Stickers Sauce

⅓ cup thin soy sauce

⅓ cup rice wine vinegar

⅓ cup sliced scallions

1 teaspoon sesame oil

1 teaspoon Sriracha

Index